Anonymous

Sylvan Scenes Along the Line of the Philadelphia and

Reading Railroad

Anonymous

Sylvan Scenes Along the Line of the Philadelphia and Reading Railroad

ISBN/EAN: 9783337419530

Printed in Europe, USA, Canada, Australia, Japan

Cover: Foto ©Andreas Hilbeck / pixelio.de

More available books at **www.hansebooks.com**

SYLVAN SCENES

---THE---
GUARANTEE TRUST
—AND—
SAFE DEPOSIT COMPANY.

CAPITAL, - - $1,000,000.

Nos. 316, 318 and 320 Chestnut Street, Philadelphia.

Rents Safes in its Fire and Burglar Proof Vaults (which are protected by Six Hall Double Chronometer Time Locks, with non-lockout attachment), with Combination and Permutation Locks, that can only be opened by the renter, at from $7 to $125 per year.

Allows Interest on Deposits of Money; Acts as Executor, Administrator, Guardian, Assignee, Committee, Receiver, Agent, Attorney, etc., etc., and Executes Trusts of every kind under appointment of States, Courts, Corporations, or Individuals, **Holding Trust Funds Separate and Apart from the Assets of the Company.**

Collects Interest on Income, and transacts all other business authorized by its Charter.

Receives for Safe Keeping, under guarantee, Valuables of every description, such as Coupon and Registered Bonds, Certificates of Stock, Deeds, Mortgages, Coin, Silverware, Jewelry, etc.

Acts as Registrar or Transfer Agent of Railroad, Mining and other Corporation Stocks and Bonds. Receipts for and Safely Keeps Wills without Charge.

Especial attention is called to our Vaults for the Storage and Safe Keeping of large packages of SILVERWARE and other valuables in bulk, for the Summer or longer, our facilities for handling such being unsurpassed.

For FURTHER INFORMATION call at the OFFICE, or send for a CIRCULAR.

THOMAS COCHRAN, President; EDWARD C. KNIGHT, Vice-President; HARRY J. DELANY, Treasurer; JOHN JAY GILROY, Secretary; RICHARD C. WINSHIP, Trust Officer.

DIRECTORS. —Thomas Cochran, Edward C. Knight, J. Barlow Moorhead, Thomas MacKellar, John J. Stadiger, Clayton French, W. Rotch Wister, Alfred Fitler, J. Dickinson Sergeant, Aaron Fries, Charles A. Sparks, Joseph Moore, Jr , Richard Y. Cook.

SYLVAN SCENES

ALONG THE LINE

OF THE

V

PHILADELPHIA AND READING

RAILROAD

WITH ILLUSTRATIONS ON WOOD FROM DRAWINGS BY EMINENT ARTISTS

REVISED BY THE PASSENGER DEPARTMENT

OF THE

PHILADELPHIA AND READING RAILROAD

1889

nsurance Company of North America,

232 WALNUT STREET, PHILADELPHIA.

ORGANIZED 1792. INCORPORATED 1794.

FIRE, MARINE and INLAND INSURANCE.

ONE HUNDRED AND NINETIETH SEMI-ANNUAL STATEMENT
OF THE ASSETS OF THE COMPANY:

Capital Stock,	$3,000,000 00
Reserve for Re-Insurance,	2,820,733 92
Reserve for Unadjusted Losses and other Liabilities,	237,315 99
Surplus over all Liabilities,	2,638,906 65

Total Assets, January 1, 1889, - - $8,696,956 56

CHARLES PLATT, President.   T. CHARLTON HENRY, Vice-President.
WILLIAM A. PLATT, 2d Vice-President.   GREVILLE E. FRYER, Secretary.
EUGENE L. ELLISON, Assistant Secretary.

SUPERB LAGER BEER.—SPECIAL BREWINGS
FOR BOTTLING AND EXPORT.

UNRIVALED PORTER, ALES and BROWN STOUT

Gold Medal and Certificates of Award of "First Degree of Merit," for "INDIA PALE ALE," in wood, for Brilliancy, Soundness of Taste, Body and Strength, and for "BROWN STOUT," in wood, for its Superiority over Competitors, at the World's Industrial and Cotton Centennial Exposition, New Orleans, 1885.

JOHN F. BETZ & SON, ADDRESS: CROWN, WILLOW AND FIFTH STS. PHILADELPHIA.

F. A. HOYT & CO.

1026

• • ○ • • CHESTNUT STREET, • • • •

PHILADELPHIA.

Clothing ✳ Ready Made

AND ALSO MADE TO ORDER FOR

BOYS AND YOUNG MEN.

Merchant Tailors.

BUSINESS SUITS MADE TO ORDER AT POPULAR PRICES.

✢ LADIES' JACKETS ✢

SACQUES ·AND· RIDING HABITS

MADE TO ORDER.

SYLVAN SCENES.

PHILADELPHIA AND READING DEPOT AT READING, PA.

WHILE the major portion of the residents of this section of the country are familiar with the name of the Philadelphia and Reading Railroad, yet very few fully realize the magnitude or importance of that Company. The position it occupies as the means of transportation can partially be appreciated, when it is stated that the system comprises two thousand and eighty-seven miles of track, penetrating the richest mineral and agricultural region on the continent; that the Company runs six hundred and forty-six passenger trains daily, in addition to the innumerable coal and freight trains, and transports annually upwards of 16,000,000 passengers and 25,000,000 tons of freight.

Originally constructed with a view to the transportation of coal from the great anthracite fields of Pennsylvania to tide-water, this road has developed into one of the most complete, powerful and efficient railway systems in the United States.

The Company was incorporated in 1833, and that portion of the line extending from Reading to Philadelphia (fifty-eight miles) was completed in 1839; the first train passing over it on

December 5th of the latter year. From this humble beginning the present magnificent system has grown by successive extensions and acquisitions; and to-day the Reading Railroad stands foremost among the great railroad companies of America.

Its main line reaches from Philadelphia to Williamsport, two hundred miles, with numerous branches diverging to Allentown,

TUNNEL AT PHŒNIXVILLE, PA.

Lancaster, Harrisburg and other prominent cities; and, in the Mahanoy and Schuylkill coal basins, the road forms an elaborate network of lines, which tap every portion of this famous coal and iron territory. Connecting at Williamsport with the Vanderbilt system of roads, it carries the immense traffic of that vast combination of lines to and from Philadelphia.

VALLEY FORGE.

WASHINGTON'S HEAD QUARTERS.

A branch of the Reading, fifty-six miles long, known as the Bethlehem Branch (formerly the North Pennsylvania Railroad), runs from Philadelphia to Bethlehem, connecting at the latter point with the

Central Railroad of New Jersey and with the Erie-Lehigh Valley lines and their affiliated systems in the West and in Canada.

The New York Division, in conjunction with the Central Railroad of New Jersey, forms the far-famed and justly celebrated

READING, PA

New York and Philadelphia New Line, sometimes called the Bound Brook Route. On this division the business of transporting human freight has been brought to its highest development; as in construction, equipment and general excellence of

SAMUEL W. BELL, President.
HENRY C. STROUD, Cashier.

JOHN MASON, Transfer Officer.
WILLIE RUSHTON, Asst. Cashier.

THE FARMERS

——AND——

MECHANICS NATIONAL BANK

PHILADELPHIA.

ARTICLES OF ASSOCIATION,

17th of January, A. D. 1807.

CHARTERED,

16th of March, A. D. 1809.

Re-Chartered:
| 25th of March, A. D. 1824.
| 18th of April, A. D. 1843.
| 16th of March, A. D. 1849.
| 24th of April, A. D. 1856.

ORGANIZED UNDER THE NATIONAL BANK ACT OF 1864,

20th OF OCTOBER, A. D. 1864.

Appointed Loan and Transfer Agent of the Commonwealth of Pennsylvania, April 21st, 1858.

Appointed Agent for Philadelphia Clearing House Association, February 1st, 1858.

Appointed Loan and Transfer Agent of the City of Philadelphia, February 16th, 1872.

HARRISBURG, PA.

service, it ranks as
one of the finest lines
of railway in the world.
At its New York terminus,
connections are made with
the rail and boat lines for all
points in the New England States.

The Reading Railroad thus occupies a position of commanding importance in its relations to the trunk lines; and its influence, in questions effecting through traffic, is correspondingly great. But while its through business is of considerable volume, the unvarying policy of the Company has been to foster and promote its local business; and the wisdom of such policy, persistently enforced, is demonstrated by the enviable condition of its local business on the Germantown and Norristown Branch, Bethlehem Branch and New York Branch. Philadelphia is not only the seat of enormous manufacturing industries, but is also the commercial centre of a vast and highly productive

BROOKSIDE, PA.

tributary territory, and is also peculiarly blest in its surroundings. Many thousands of the persons engaged in various pursuits in the city make their homes in the beautiful suburbs that lie to the northward of Philadelphia; and the daily transportation of this class constitutes a highly important and remunerative feature of the Reading's business. One of the divisions which has occupied considerable attention of the Company

recently has been the New Jersey Division, which connects Philadelphia with Atlantic City, the largest and most celebrated sea-side
resort in America.   The main line of this division is frequently
designated "The Atlantic City Short Line," on account of being the

POTTSVILLE, PA.

most direct route to the queen of sea-side pleasuring places.   The
branches of this division and their direct connections reach the chief
commercial and manufacturing centres of Southern New Jersey.

Besides tapping a territory comprising many large and prosperous manufacturing cities and towns and the rich mineral and

agricultural regions, the Reading's lines reach a large variety
of picturesque pleasure places, which, owing to their admirable
location, easy accessibility, and by virtue of their many natural
beauties and advantages, render them dear to many as places of

ALLENTOWN, PA.

recreation or on account of their invigorating and health-giving
climates. Among these places are the numerous sea-side resorts
that are located along the New Jersey coast, the most prominent
of which is Atlantic City, that peerless and charming city by
the sea. Atlantic City for many years was known only as a
summer resort; but, of late years, the medical fraternity, the
invalid and persons desirous of relaxation from the cares of
business or the social whirl, have begun to recognize the superior
claims of the city as a winter resort and sanitarium; and now
many thousands migrate to this popular pleasuring place during

both the winter and summer seasons, and all pay tribute to its many charms and beauties, and testify to the fact that no better sanitarium can be found than exists here.

Those who prefer the mountains to the sea-shore can readily find a spot to suit them in the mountainous district penetrated by the Reading Railroad, no matter how fastidious their tastes may be. The Schuylkill and Mahanoy regions, traversed by this

BETHLEHEM
FROM LEHIGH UNIVERSITY.

line, contain many localities dedicated almost exclusively to pleasure seekers. The most noted of these resorts are Eagle's Mere and

Highland Lake, situated on a spur of the great Alleghenies; the former in Sullivan county and the latter in Lycoming county. This territory was until recently unknown to the pleasure tourist; but, once having been invaded, it at once became very popular, owing to the magnificence of the scenery, the diversified means

LANCASTER, PA.

of recreation and the health-giving properties of the atmosphere, which is permeated with the invigorating fragrance of the pine and hemlock trees which abound in this country.

Then again there are many who have a preference for suburban life. To such we would say, that the most charming of rural spots in Eastern Pennsylvania are located along the lines of the Philadelphia and Reading Railroad. The territory traversed by the Bethlehem Branch, New York Branch, and the Germantown and Norristown Branches, are particularly adapted for out-of-town homes. The country along these branches is already becoming thickly populated by those who have recognized the benefits accruing to a home beyond the turmoil of a large city. The Company, in order to keep pace with its constantly increasing

LOCK HAVEN, PA.

local traffic, has been continually augmenting its train facilities, until at present the service comprises trains to and from points on each of these branches every few minutes in the day.

The equipment in service on all the divisions of the Reading Railroad is the finest obtainable, and the employés of the road are at all times respectful and attentive, thus insuring to the traveler fast time, comfortable and even luxurious accommodations

WILLIAMSPORT, PA.

and courteous consideration. The officials of the Company have pursued the most liberal policy in the management of the great property in their control, and the result of such policy is clearly indicated by the superior condition of its roadway, magnificence of equipment, and the admirable and efficient system in vogue in the transaction of its business. The road is laid with the best and heaviest steel rails, on first-class ties, embedded in stone and cinder ballast. The rolling stock in the passenger service is composed of coaches

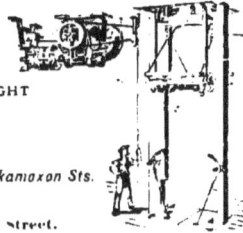

of the finest and most improved construction, replete with all the luxurious appointments known to modern railroad car building. The road also has in service every danger-lessening device known to science ; and passengers via the Philadelphia and Reading Line can seat themselves in one of the magnificent

PACIFIC AVENUE, ATLANTIC CITY, N J.

coaches and feel assured that they will reach their destination in perfect safety. Another excellent feature of the Reading Road is the quick time made on its lines. The fastest time ever made on any railroad in the world was made on the Philadelphia and Reading Railroad's New York Line, when ninety-two miles was run in ninety-three minutes ; one mile being made in forty-six seconds. While the trains do not usually run at this tremendous high rate of speed, yet the road still maintains a train service that cannot be excelled in speed or general efficience.

How glad we feel when we can truly and heartily say that the summer has come at last in all its plenitude of light and warmth, and that out of doors everything is rich in fragrance! fragrance exquisite! of new-mown hay, of wild thyme, dewy washed. What hopes we had built upon its advent. To us it means forgetfulness of winter, the chilling frost, and snow, and

ATLANTIC CITY, N. J.

suffering. It means that the fickle days of spring are gone also. Summer means liberty, romping, frolic, fun; breakfasting with open windows, and with the song of birds echoing through the house or the cozy tent. It means pleasant saunterings in the open air, in the woods, by the sea-shore, among the mountains, everywhere enjoying life to the full. It means the early morning walk in the dewy forest, when the shafts of light look wet and green; and long lingering in the garden at night, when the "mild twilight, like a silver clasp, unites to-day with yesterday,

SUNBURY, PA.

and Morning and Evening sit together, hand in hand, beneath the starless sky of midnight." The woods are just now in their fullest leaf. These days have come, but these days will go. The chequered tints of autumn will all too quickly make their appearance. So let us make the most of these green fields and mountain nooks; these country pleasures, and fleeting marvels of sweet Nature in her happiest and loveliest moods. If we need rest, let us seek it where it is freely offered, and where it may be found. Let us enjoy the glad summer while it lasts and feel the infinite bliss of nature throbbing in every vein.

When the sweet breath of May steals in through the open casement, the weary clerk jumps down from his stool, the editor throws down his quill, the merchant forgets his ledger, the city clergyman asks for his vacation, the lawyer grows weary of the court-room, and each, packing up his valise, draws a long breath, heaves a sigh—the pent-up feelings of a long winter's toil—and exclaims in a tone that admits of no doubt or denial, "I must get away from work ; I must go on a summer excursion." And so they must, and will. But then comes up the all-important query, "Where shall we go?" Go where nature offers a mingling of the accessible and picturesque, the secluded haunts in wood and dell, where we can see the branches of the trees bend down our touch to meet, and the clover-blossoms in the grass rise up to kiss our feet.

MAUCH CHUNK.

M AUCH CHUNK. A place noted alike for its wild, picturesque
scenery, its salubrious atmosphere, and its popularity as
a pleasure resort. Here Nature's elements appear to have waged
their fiercest warfare. Here the Lehigh met its boldest obstruc-
tions—whole ranges of mountains hurled themselves directly in

its path, threatening to bar its further progress, among which it madly sweeps, or, cutting them in twain, dashes onward to the sea,—here, where the struggle was fiercest, where the stream doubles and turns in its mad efforts to escape, rasping the mountains to their rocky foundation, overshadowed by their

VIEW NORTH FROM MT. PISGAH.

towering heights, lies the picturesque village of Mauch Chunk; its Swiss-like cottages clinging to the mountains, which threaten every moment to topple them over into the turbid river below. At the Mansion House, which stands invitingly at the entrance of the village, the guests may step from the second or third

stories to the vine-clad hills in the rear, behind which the sun is
hidden early in the afternoon. Aside from the cool salubrious
atmosphere, the attractions of the Lehigh Valley are many and
interesting. The *Switchback Railroad* is one of the most novel.
This is one of the great objective points. The whole scene is

VIEW SOUTH FROM MT. PISGAH.

characterized by novelty and excitement. Ladies should prepare
themselves with an extra wrap, to guard against the effect of the
fresh breeze as the cars skim along the mountain side. Another
feature is the visit to *Glen Onoko*. Each year new improvements
are made, to develop the attractions of this already famous resort.

Thousands of dollars have been expended; well-graded paths, with rustic steps and bridges, wind up the narrow valley, crossing and recrossing the stream, which, by successive leaps, comes coursing down the mountain side; now stealing among the rocks, overhung by clinging vines, or the bright flowers and shining

IN THE MOUNTAINS.

leaves of the rhododendron; now dashing madly down some rocky cliffs, a charming cascade, or more imposing waterfall. A more picturesque spot cannot be found. Below Onoko station is a high bluff, through which the Lehigh and Susquehanna Division of the Central Railroad of New Jersey passes by tunnel. It is

BEAR MOUNTAIN.

GLEN ONOKO.

properly known as Moyer's Rock, and possesses a traditional interest. The story is told in this wise: During the early settlement of the country, a noted hunter and Indian fighter living in

SWITCHBACK.

Mahoning Valley, four miles
south, who had hitherto eluded
all attempts at capture, was surrounded, taken prisoner, and
disarmed, by five Indian warriors, and left on the summit of this
rock for security, guarded by two of their number, while the
others hunted for game. Moyer was sorely perplexed. To fight
alone two armed Indians was not to be thought of; and long he
pondered. Suddenly starting he listened intently, then relaxed

PROSPECT PARK.

into his former quiet. The Indians watched him unmoved. Again he started; and, creeping to the very brink, throwing into his countenance all the interest he could command, he gazed intently down. The ruse succeeded: overcome by curiosity, the Indians unguardedly moved to his side, and sought to discover the interest, when, with the spring of the tiger, he seized and dashed them to the rocks below.

The visitor to *Glen Onoko* should be well shod, as well as suitably clothed, the refreshing coolness of the atmosphere rendering the extra wrap acceptable here as well as when going over the

Switchback. The successive cascades, waterfalls, and other objects of interest at Glen Onoko have each received appropriate names, and are worthy an individual description; but details must be left to local guides. This brief sketch can but give a passing notice. The entire Glen is a striking freak of nature, and reveals pictures of grandeur and magnificence not often excelled. Near the top

SCRANTON, PA.

of the Glen, some nine hundred feet above the Lehigh, runs the old *Warrior Path*, being the war-trail used, it may be for centuries, by the Indians in passing from the Susquehanna to the Delaware. It was also traversed by General Sullivan and his brave army after the bloody Wyoming massacre in the year 1778, and subsequently by the lumberman in plying his trade, whence it was known as the *Raftsman's Path*.

GLEN SUMMIT.

Cannot we spend a day at Upper Lehigh? "Where's that?" asks the reader. We answer: "Up among the mountains. Among the woods. Splendid scenery—rocks, ravines, cascades, good hotel, good fishing——" "That'll do! Let's start!" Next

WYOMING VALLEY AND WILKE-BARRE.

morning be-
fore the sun
is up, we are
astir. It is worth getting
up to see a sunrise among
the Lehigh Mountains. We
ate our breakfast, went to
White Haven, changed cars
and rode up the Nescopeck
Railroad to Upper Lehigh.

When we reached the place we walked about half a mile
along a wood-road, struck into a footpath, followed it a hundred
yards or so, and without warning, walked out on a flat rock

VIEW NEAR RAMAPO STATION.

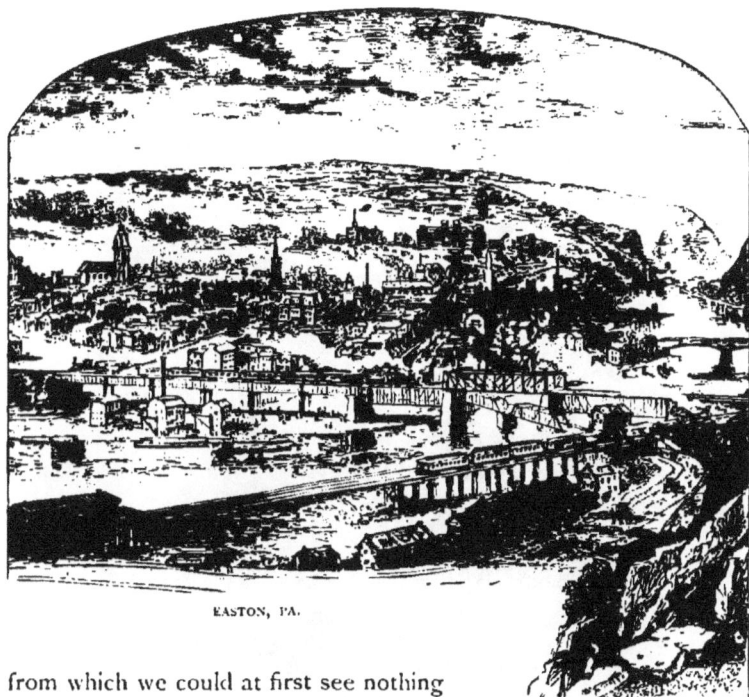

EASTON, PA.

from which we could at first see nothing
but fog, up, down or around.   It was
a misty morning, but we made out to understand that we were
on the verge of a precipice which fell sheer down into a
tremendous abyss; and when the fog lifted, as it did about noon,
we looked out upon miles and miles of valleys partly cleared,
but principally covered with the primeval forest.

We were on Prospect Rock then. Presently our guide took
us, by a roundabout way, to Cloud Point, a corresponding pro-
jection, on the other side of the Glen, and here a still wider
view lay before us. We gazed on the beautiful landscape until
we thought we could afford to leave it for a while, and then
descended into Glen Thomas, so called in honor of David Thomas,

the pioneer of the iron trade of the Lehigh. It was the first of May, but we found here miniature glaciers formed by the water falling over the rocks, the ice three feet and more in thickness, and so solid that a pistol-ball fired at it point-blank rebounded as from a rock, while not a hundred yards away May flowers were blooming in fragrant abundance.

But I cannot remain even in this beautiful place. I must on. I may not tell of our carriage ride into the Mahoning Valley, with its pleasant views and drives; nor of mountain climbing at Mauch

Chunk; nor of the flying visit we paid to Wilkesbarre and Scranton in the beautiful Wyoming Valley; nor of the day we spent in the quaint and pleasant Moravian town of Bethlehem. All these things must remain untold, but the reader can enjoy them all for himself at small cost of time or money. He can see the Lehigh Valley, Switchback and all, in a single day, returning to Philadelphia the same evening, or he can spend a whole summer in exploring the woods and mountains of this delightful region.

His best plan, however, for a short trip, is to leave Philadelphia or New York on the early train, timing himself so that he can be at the Mansion House, Mauch Chunk, in time for dinner. After dinner he will have plenty of time to go over the Gravity Road and return in time for supper. Next morning an early train will take him to White Haven, where he can change cars and run up the Nescopeck Road to Upper Lehigh, which he will reach about noon. Here he will have ample time to dine and explore Glen Thomas, but not to see all the fine views from this singular mountain-top, if he would return by the afternoon train. This train makes connections for both Philadelphia and New York, either of which can be reached the same evening ; but a third day can be profitably spent at Upper Lehigh, and part of a fourth in exploring Glen Onoko, one of the greatest attractions about Mauch Chunk, but accessible from that place only on foot. It demands a hard walk and a hard climb, but offers in return a scene of wild and rugged magnificence which in all mountain climbing has never been excelled.

No tourist should fail to see this most extraordinary glen. Its ever varying beauties may be gazed on for hours, as one would gaze entranced on a moving panorama, unmindful of all else, and regardless of the lapse of time.

WINTER-SUMMER LANDS.

"KNOW thyself," said the ancient sage. "Know thy country," with equal wisdom says the modern philosopher. Who is there that knows it?—that has viewed its wonders from the

Sunny South to the ice-bound North?—from the populous regions of the East to the vast plains, mountains and valleys of the great West? Like an invading host Americans rush to Europe, to enjoy the picturesque and the sublime, unmindful of the fact

that at their doors are beauties unsurpassed—rolling hills and dales, lakes, seas and rivers, mountains, valleys, fields and woods, charming landscapes, picturesqueness and sublimity, just as the Creator has fashioned the elements. The host from

America are met by an ever-increasing host from Europe, who wisely recognize the magnificent resources of a country which has already surpassed all others. It offers endless variety of scenery to charm and interest the eye and mind.

Putting aside for a time North, East and West, there is a new region, which is known as the great Southwest, a land flowing with milk and honey, partaking of all the charming qualities of the Sunny South, and yet possessing unique advantages of its own. It is distinctively the land of the magnificent—a new empire which stretches to the Gulf of Mexico and the country of the Aztecs, and unlimited in natural resources, varied in soil, abounding in wealth hitherto undreamed of, in superb scenery and delightful climate. To any one who has never traveled through the Southwest, it is like entering an undiscovered country. Not a moment passes that something interesting is not presented to view. Nature has been lavish in her gifts to the soil, and man has followed the bent of Nature's mood. The immense ranches and ranges on which thousands of cattle graze, the vast farms and plantations, the thriving cities which seem to have sprung from the ground

in a day, give evidence of the wealth and enterprise which prevail everywhere. The State of Texas is an empire in itself, which, on the ruins of an old and unprogressive civilization, has built up a vast people, with prosperous and varied industries, and this, too, within a dozen years. With an area larger than that of France or the German Empire, and capable of supporting

as many persons as the entire
United States now contains, it has
a soil which can duplicate everything grown in this country, a
climate which varies from the temperate to the semi-tropical, and
scenery which includes every kind of natural landscape. It is
the charming climate of Central and Southern Texas which is
bringing the State into prominence as a pleasure resort for all,
and a recuperating land for those in delicate health. Its shores
are lapped by the waters of the Gulf, from the broad bosom of
which refreshing breezes blow, tempering the heat of the sun.
In winter the atmosphere is never more than mildly bracing;
and, when the northern portions of the country are locked in
ice and snow, balmy winds are blowing and flowers are blooming

in this land of sunshine. To the passing visitor there is on every side an endless series of interesting and instructive objects.

Let any one who would find rare enjoyment take a trip through the Southwest. He will never regret it. Every convenience of modern travel may be obtained. Luxurious Pullman buffet coaches run through from St. Louis to all the principal points in Texas, over the Missouri Pacific or the Iron Mountain Railway.

By the former the route lies through the heart of Missouri, revealing the picturesque country that lies adjacent to St. Louis in the valley of the Merrimac, and then sweeping along the majestic and turbulent Missouri, with bluffs and rolling country

on one side and rich alluvial soil on the other. After leaving
the river the road runs into the cultivated prairie due west, until
Sedalia is reached. Then, without change, the coach is attached

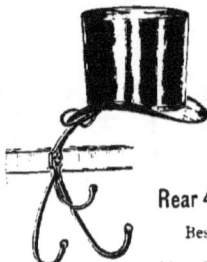

to the Missouri, Kansas and Texas, and the journey toward the
Sunny South is commenced. After running through the thriving
towns and rapidly developing country of Southwestern Missouri,
the road passes through a corner of Kansas, and then rushes
into Indian Territory. The road traverses this magnificent strip
of land to its southern boundary, disclosing interesting views
of the civilization which has been grafted in the aboriginal races.
Phases of life and passing glances of races, which in many

respects are fascinating, are obtained in this way only. There
is no other route which passes through the heart of Indian
Territory and offers opportunity to see the aboriginal people in
their homes and under their own government. A trip over this
road will bring the traveler to parts in the South where it seems
as if a magic wand had been passed over the country, transforming
nature in its wildest state into populous cities and prosperous
towns, putting railroads where there were only savage trails, and

building, as in a day, all the evidences of high modern civilization, with its industries, schools and beautiful homes.

Let us glance briefly at this southern land. Running through Fort Worth, Waco, and many smaller towns, we come to the International and Great Northern, which leads to the Rio Grande and the Mexican border. There is exquisite scenery on the line of the road which fills the eye with beauty. One of the curiosities of nature, duplicating the wonderful natural bridge of Virginia, is a natural bridge in Rockwell county, under which a clear stream bubbles over mossy rocks, forming deep pools, where the finest fish may be caught. Here, when snow and ice are the proper things in the Northern States, the farmers may be seen preparing the land for the spring crops. On the International the most beautiful scenery is presented to view, with the surface rolling and broken in places, but frequently smooth, and abounding in natural vegetation. Austin, a short distance beyond Taylor, is a charming city. It is surrounded by rich farming lands, and it has many beautiful residences, situated on lofty eminences. Being the capital of the State, it is the centre of social distinction. There are magnificent public buildings, one of the finest hotels (the Driskill) in the country, and the capitol, which is in course of erection, will be surpassed in cost and grandeur

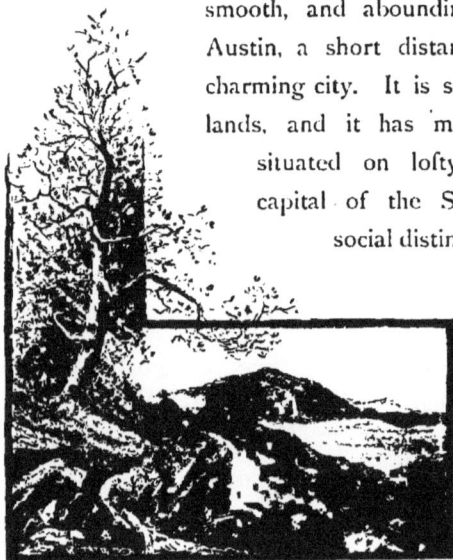

only by the superb structure at Albany, New York. The State University is also located here, and, with the Colorado River flowing by it, the city is full of interest.

Going further south, historic San Antonio is reached. Here the progressive civilization of America meets the quaint civilization of the Aztecs and the Spaniards. There, too, are blended in San Antonio the adobe and the stone and iron fronts hobnobbing together. There is, perhaps, no city which is more fascinating to the traveler than San Antonio. It is surrounded by a beautiful country, made picturesque by the shining thread of the San Pedro River. The town itself is quaint and pretty, with its ancient churches presenting types of architecture which are singularly picturesque and in strong contrast with the modern buildings of the American population. Here a genuine touch of Mexican life is given in the people and the homes. Chief, however, in charm is the Alamo, the shrine of Texan independence, where the blood of heroes was spilled for liberty. The high location of the city, with its mild, bracing air and delightful climate, make it admirable and popular for all in delicate health. When one cannot live elsewhere, he can enjoy life at San Antonio, and thousands of invalids go there every winter, and even in summer (the nights

being always cool) for the benefit of their health. From this point the road runs to Laredo and the Rio Grande.

Running from Denison by the east branch of the road, the same evidence of natural beauty and resources is found on every hand. Palestine one of the wonders of the State in the way of rapid growth is passed, and then the land begins to slope toward the Gulf of Mexico. The entire aspect of the country changes, and, after Houston is passed, the traveler is in the rich and fertile lowlands of the extreme South.

This is the land of corn, sugar-cane and cotton, and is not without its interesting qualities. At the end of the trip, however, is a treat in the beautiful "Oleander City"—Galveston—with its magnificent harbor, where the stately ships ride at anchor, and where is the finest beach in America. The lovely waters of the Gulf make soft and swelling music for Galveston, and the gentle, spice-laden breeze, that blows over its shining bosom, cools and refreshes weary humanity in midsummer; while in winter, if such a season can be mentioned, the same breeze blows balmy and warmth-giving from the waters which sweep around the world

and tempers the climate of other and bleaker shores. Galveston is a garden where flowers ever bloom, and it is filled with wealth and refinement. No pleasanter resort to escape the rigors of a Northern winter can be found.

An interesting trip is that through Western Texas, over the Texas and Pacific Rai road. The road is tapped at Longview by the Iron Mountain, and at Fort Worth by the Missouri,

Kansas and Texas, so that either route is equally convenient. Going west, however, over nearly the entire breadth of the State, gives one a splendid idea not only of its vast area, but also of the character of the country. A short distance west of Fort Worth, the Brazos River is crossed, and the train rushes through high, rolling prairies, broken here and there with growths of oak, ash, pecan, hickory and walnut, and, on the hill-sides, cedar. As the journey progresses west the timber becomes smaller, except in the valleys and on the loftier eminences, where tall pines and

cedars grow.. There are elevations where magnificent views of characteristic Texas landscapes may be obtained. Mesquite may be seen in abundance. The scenery becomes more of a distinct type, and interesting vistas pass before the eye at every turn. It is here that nature is found in its primitive state, with the exception of the settlements which are found along the line. At the Pecos River an entirely different land formation, and one which is exceedingly curious and interesting, commences. Here the extreme base of the Rocky Mountains begins, and it rises northwestwardly—not gradually, at a gentle slope, but by enormous steps. It is the grand stairway to the sublime peaks that divide the continent. The huge steps are from fifty to five hundred feet high, and the plateaux above extend from fifty to one hundred miles on a level, until another and higher plain is reached. The level surface above each step forms beautiful valleys or coves, which are protected from the cold winds that come from the north and west. The train climbs the Sierra Blanco Mountains until an elevation of five thousand feet is gained. From this lofty point, and through picturesque surroundings, the road sweeps down to El Paso, the gateway to old Mexico.

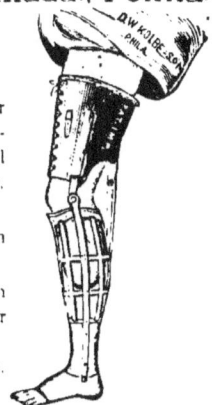

The Chalfonte.

ON THE BEACH.
FIRST-CLASS IN ALL APPOINTMENTS.

SALT-WATER BATHS IN THE HOUSE.   *CIRCULARS ON APPLICATION.*

E. ROBERTS & SONS,
ATLANTIC CITY, N. J.

ATLANTIC CITY.

THE WELLINGTON.   *Open all the Year.*

Ocean End Kentucky Avenue.

FULL OCEAN VIEW.   **A. B. HUNTER.**

HADDON HALL,

Sea End of North Carolina Avenue,

EDWIN LIPPINCOTT.   ATLANTIC CITY, N. J.

LEHIGH VALLEY RAILROAD.

The Great Pleasure-Travel Route.

THE SHORTEST, QUICKEST AND MOST DESIRABLE ROUTE TO

ALLENTOWN,	WHITE HAVEN,	TAUGHANNOCK FALLS,
CATASAUQUA,	GLEN SUMMIT,	WATKINS' GLEN,
COPLAY,	WILKESBARRE,	BUFFALO,
SLATINGTON,	PITTSTON,	NIAGARA FALLS,
LEHIGHTON,	AUBURN,	THOUSAND ISLANDS,
MAUCH CHUNK,	ITHACA,	SARATOGA,
GLEN ONOKO,	GENEVA,	THE ADIRONDACKS,

THE SWITCHBACK, and Points in the LEHIGH and WYOMING VALLEYS,
and NORTHERN and WESTERN NEW YORK.

ALSO, ALL POPULAR WATERING-PLACES OF THE NORTH.

THROUGH TRAINS.

PULLMAN PALACE SLEEPING CARS.

✦ FOR POINTS IN THE VALLEY OF THE LEHIGH. ✦

TICKET OFFICES:

NEW YORK:

General Eastern Office, 235 Broadway.

Depot Foot of Courtland Street.   *Depot foot of Desbrosses Street.*

All Penn'a R. R. Ticket Offices, and Dodd's Transfer Co.'s Offices.

PHILADELPHIA:

Lehigh Valley R. R. Ticket Office, 836 Chestnut Street.

624 Chestnut Street.

P. & R. Depot, Third and Berks Streets.   *P. & R. Depot, Ninth and Green Streets.*

BUFFALO:

Corner Main and Seneca Streets.

N. VAN HORN,   E. B. BYINGTON,

Gen'l S. E. Pass. Agent.   *Gen'l Pass. Agent.*